Shy Lands

Poems by
Diane Jarvenpa

BLUE LIGHT PRESS ◆ 1ST WORLD PUBLISHING

SAN FRANCISCO ◆ FAIRFIELD ◆ DELHI

Shy Lands

Copyright ©2023, Diane Jarvenpa

All rights reserved. Printed in the United States of America. No part of this book may be used or reproduced in any manner whatsoever without written permission except in the case of brief quotations embodied in critical articles and reviews. For information contact:

BLUE LIGHT PRESS
www.bluelightpress.com
bluelightpress@aol.com

1ST WORLD PUBLISHING
PO Box 2211
Fairfield, IA 52556
www.1stworldpublishing.com

BOOK & COVER DESIGN
Melanie Gendron
melaniegendron999@gmail.com

COVER ART
Imaginary Landscape with Blue Lines by Lelde Kalmite

AUTHOR PHOTO
LiLi Jarvenpa

FIRST EDITION

Library of Congress Cataloging-in-Publication Data

ISBN: 978-1-4218-3533-4

Praise for *Shy Lands*

There is a subtle and proficient music in Diane Jarvenpa's poems. They derive their power from how deeply she sees and listens to herself and to the earth. In *Shy Lands* she welcomes us into a world quite similar to her description of her mother's garden, its "precision of beauty, intricate storytelling, a knowledge of what blends, what harmonizes, what stands alone." And we become aware that despite the sorrow and anguish we might feel about the hell that humans have made of much of our natural world, we can still immerse ourselves in what has not been lost. Her poems remind us that we can find solace and belonging in that "light" and "articulate wonder" which can "fit so completely into the grooves of all our shadows." We can both celebrate and grieve earth's wonders, those which are extinct and those which are gloriously still with us – if we immerse ourselves in the natural world and "let it enter and grow in our bodies."

– Freya Manfred, author of *Loon in Late November Water*

While Diane Jarvenpa is a self-described shy person from a shy family in a shy land, she is a fierce poet. Jarvenpa's new book, *Shy Lands*, describes an imaginatively-animated world, a quiet family in the background, all the elements of nature which the poet has observed, consumed, and returned to the reader in another form through some exercise of magical alchemy. As I was reading her manuscript, I made notes in the margin – *"Beautiful!"* – *"Beautiful!"* – until I figured I should come up with a word other than – *"Beautiful."* So here's the word – *"Transformational"*. I have been transformed by these poems which is what great poetry does. *Praise and Transform.* Jarvenpa praises everything within her considerable range – "stamps, maps, lily pads," " "a comet or a wild fire." The old dog – "She is your teacher now./Scholar with tail,/Athena with canines." *Shy Lands*, the country Diane Jarvenpa inhabits, the country we all inhabit, is ravaged and threatened, but still, with her power to convert the observed into a "cold wild song," she finds for all of us some kind of inspired redemption.

– Tim Nolan, author of *Lines*

Diane Jarvenpa's latest collection, *Shy Lands*, teaches us how to engage the natural world with the careful listening of an introvert, "pushed by the wind…hearing the drops of dew." Her attention draws us to the tiny things that make up a whole landscape, and that, she tells us, "is where the village of [her] mind has brought [her]." She uses words the way an impressionist painter deploys color, "know[ing] how all this works, the close and the distant, / the heap and faded, / the swoop and the click." This new beauty is only possible in a shy and quiet land, the one she creates for us here.

– Joyce Sutphen, author of *Carrying Water to the Field*

Praise for *Shy Lands*

There is a subtle and proficient music in Diane Jarvenpa's poems. They derive their power from how deeply she sees and listens to herself and to the earth. In *Shy Lands* she welcomes us into a world quite similar to her description of her mother's garden, its "precision of beauty, intricate storytelling, a knowledge of what blends, what harmonizes, what stands alone." And we become aware that despite the sorrow and anguish we might feel about the hell that humans have made of much of our natural world, we can still immerse ourselves in what has not been lost. Her poems remind us that we can find solace and belonging in that "light" and "articulate wonder" which can "fit so completely into the grooves of all our shadows." We can both celebrate and grieve earth's wonders, those which are extinct and those which are gloriously still with us – if we immerse ourselves in the natural world and "let it enter and grow in our bodies."

– Freya Manfred, author of *Loon in Late November Water*

While Diane Jarvenpa is a self-described shy person from a shy family in a shy land, she is a fierce poet. Jarvenpa's new book, *Shy Lands*, describes an imaginatively-animated world, a quiet family in the background, all the elements of nature which the poet has observed, consumed, and returned to the reader in another form through some exercise of magical alchemy. As I was reading her manuscript, I made notes in the margin – *"Beautiful!"* – *"Beautiful!* – until I figured I should come up with a word other than – *"Beautiful."* So here's the word – *"Transformational"*. I have been transformed by these poems which is what great poetry does. *Praise and Transform.* Jarvenpa praises everything within her considerable range – "stamps, maps, lily pads," "a comet or a wild fire." The old dog – "She is your teacher now./Scholar with tail,/Athena with canines." *Shy Lands*, the country Diane Jarvenpa inhabits, the country we all inhabit, is ravaged and threatened, but still, with her power to convert the observed into a "cold wild song," she finds for all of us some kind of inspired redemption.

– Tim Nolan, author of *Lines*

Diane Jarvenpa's latest collection, *Shy Lands*, teaches us how to engage the natural world with the careful listening of an introvert, "pushed by the wind…hearing the drops of dew." Her attention draws us to the tiny things that make up a whole landscape, and that, she tells us, "is where the village of [her] mind has brought [her]." She uses words the way an impressionist painter deploys color, "know[ing] how all this works, the close and the distant, / the heap and faded, / the swoop and the click." This new beauty is only possible in a shy and quiet land, the one she creates for us here.

– Joyce Sutphen, author of *Carrying Water to the Field*

Roam about as a golden cuckoo, wander as a silver wood dove
Slip by silent as a whitefish, slide by like a fish in water
– Kalevala

If you know wilderness the way you know love,
you would be unwilling to let it go.
– Terry Tempest Willliams

Take heart. Earth feels every tremble touch. Feels each foot.
Listens now. Bring her justice, protection, peace.
– Allison Adelle Hedge Coke

Contents

I

Riding the Bubble 1
Wondering What 2
Down to Earth 4
Alive in Elegy 5
Again the Doves in the Time of the Pandemic 7
In spite of it 8
American Dream 9
It is a Flowery Revolution 10
To Shine in Answer my daughter leaves for college 11
Follow the Wild Spill 13
Equilibrium 14
Petrichor smells different on different lands 15
Haikea Longing 16

II

Ice Sings to Itself 19
Hesperia Ottoe 21
Baby Rhino 23
Map of Less 25
Tell Me About the Night Flowers 26
Too Warm for the Loon 27
Sea Glossary 28

III

Talking on the Wind Telephone 33
Surviving in a State of Denial 35
In the Office of Social Security 37
Olive Trees by Van Gogh 39
Souvenir 41
Walking an Old Dog 43
Ode to the Opposite of This 45

IV

How to Talk to Introverts 49
Libraries I Have Known 50
Petite Choses 51
Girl Monks in Quarantine 53
Cool Cool Water 55
Hermit Thrush 56
I am Boo Radley 57

V

Swim the Compass 61
The Day Has Wings 63
Shyland 64
Koivu 67
Baptism River 69

Acknowledgments 71
About the Author 73

I

The vast, wild earth. The first whip-or-u-will startles me. Hear thee.

– Henry David Thoreau

Riding the Bubble

This is the time the nucleus that formed
near the birth of the solar system
a few billion back shows up again.
Its infrared signature over the night sky,
three miles across. How do we imagine that?
Out in the deepening night, in our pockets of isolation,
staring at the stars, we lift eyes to comet smudge.
This is the business of silence. Pursuit of an echo
back to our hunting and gathering of the elusive,
its beautiful fizzing out as the new moon comes.
What is this shred of silver, nightly whisper of the past,
but a way to not feel as haunted in the full-throated dark.
A buoyant syllable scripted, should we choose to read it.
Maybe we all have a bit of flat-earther in us
when we look up, tip-toe to our own edge and gaze out.
Oh, we have flat. Let us praise stamps, maps, lily pads.
But who hasn't taken a miniature globe in hand and thought –
how improbable this puzzle of water and rock.
An apocryphal round in its extreme,
rounder than a calabash or muscadine.
Those NASA photographs of the earth make it look
like it could rupture like a bubble. And so it is,
as we are dragged again into enlightenment,
drawing back more curtains to face how humans
play pretend like nobody's business. The mind
that perceives a comet or a wildfire, a grievance or the full,
round earth doesn't have to then just turn away,
but keep perceiving it all in waves that then radiate
outward and bump into other's waves to form
some kind of silent conversation in the way trees talk,
as a way to make it all bearable, to keep practicing it
like a good old blues tune, that carries water,
that tends deep wounds, that rides a wild arc
called the future.

Wondering What

This country would look like
through the rearview mirror,
past Wall Street and its

pirate cargo hold.
What would it look like
in improbable balance?

A harvested heirloom crop
of our lost code of ethics,
a walk away from the hunger

for history sweet-frosted. Thawing
of truths packaged up nice and square
and hidden in the freezer aisle.

What would it be like to all kneel
in the garden of no border?
Bank the long beans, invest in catalpas,

mutual fund salsa with all those tomatillos,
weigh the equity narrative of the wisteria,
follow the penny diminuendo of hummingbird,

full on revenue up those blackberries,
sip every retirement fund syllable of pomegranate,
forever withdraw savings

from the jukebox of the mockingbird.
Allow that kind of liquid warbling, harm
graduated over into the transmuting light

of maybe a lily,
or penumbral moon,
a greedy hope beyond the damage.

To fall not from division or betrayal,
but fall, as in some kind of love, to tender spaces,
lush with a different kind of thunder.

Down to Earth

Robins are everywhere now, in the streets, in the elms,
dead in my hands.

The sky split and sent a male robin into the side of the house,
there in the grass, pristine,

just the way you'd find one in a natural history museum,
well-groomed, not stuffed,

but newly empty. And an instinct to will it
back to life takes over,

which chants to offer which deity, what wound
can be healed with doubt?

If I believed in reincarnation, maybe I was holding
a beautiful Bolivian farmer, Athabascan weaver,

innkeeper at the edge of Lake Baikal, or once an ant, a worm best eaten.
Who is to say connectors of worlds don't have brown wings

that settle onto a spirit tree like papery blooms?
We never know the many ghosts that hover,

how grief spurs a different calculation as we try to hold onto
a story even when it has cast off its own ending.

Hollow bones are swept back to earth
each time we bury a bird,

offered to yet one more holy landscape
where we bow down and spill our loss.

Alive in Elegy

Tucked inside a hedge
of boxwood

we picked cherries
in the south of France.

On a cloudy day,
not giboulée, but dewy air

filled with scent; limestone,
roses, kiwis swelling

on the vine. And that is where
the village of my mind

has brought me
as white petals

fall from the apple tree
all over my yard, snowing

out across the violets.
It is that same slow

speed of that other day,
mellow drumming

of cherries falling in the bucket,
how one cherry felt so warm

held in the palm, how they tasted
of meadow and wine.

How our hands and lips
stained ruby.

How our friend's garden
was a surrender of color

and how she left it behind
to keep us drunk on bees.

How that was an all pink
hemisphere, but today

it is all white and purple.
How far and close

our memories are,
how fragrant,

how hungry.

Again the Doves in the Time of the Pandemic

I have been hearing mourning doves,
what is it about their calls
that rescue a frenetic mind?

The song's slow beat insists a mellow-out
as if Donovan was singing from some rooftop
or the same way when Ray Charles offers, as only he can,

Oh What A Beautiful Morning with the Count Basie Orchestra,
there is no way you can refute that slow melodic truth.
If any directive can be found from doves

it is – make do, keep going. I do find endearing
their *Whatever man*, approach to life.
Nests made up anywhere, telephone poles will do.

But their flight, all purpose in sudden ascent or dodge,
most needed now. They survive in desert, drink brackish water,
live almost as long as Jesus, though this is unlikely.

Twenty million are hunted every year.
I find a weird hope in their returning here, a comfort in their deep
allowance for approximation. Their song sounds a lament,

maybe hunger or emergence of egg
or maybe not alarm or complaint.
I admit as I field their susurration

into my very tired brain, I nod to their sigh
of plausibility for something more than a slim wedge of hope,
for it is like Ray says, the sounds of the earth are like music.

In spite of it

blooming near a grain elevator, not far from rail-rider campsite,
    near an interstate, freeway
exhaust snaking thorns, almost lost to miniature ice age blight.

all about deliberation, slow road to bounty, blush times fragrance
    filling a clay bowl which
normally holds turnips or some kind of stew.

born from tears of Aphrodite and blood of Adonis. Nero confetti,
    hypnotizer of nightingale,
color of myth in swamp, in tundra.

spied by someone 5000 years ago who thought, I will stab myself
    and bleed in order to add
this to my life, in tea, floribunda, china, bourbon, damask, cabbage.

its water a legal tender in the 17th century. let's bring that back.
    I will give you one
1/2 milliliter of rosewater for some capons, nutmegs and jumbals.
    in honey, jelly, salt and sugar.

host to sun, rain, deer and beetles. one floret unfolds a slender
    picnic of summer, then quick
fades like in a hurry

to find the theater exit. so it goes. rose drama. a way to a song for
    some. for me, for now,
a longing, a wheel

spin in bud, pollen, petal, fruit, seed, not to forget how they break
    the rules, let
themselves be buried, how they cause such deep thirst for difficult
    dreams.

American Dream

Mine was a family of lukewarm consumers.
I was told by ardent junior high schoolers
which were the right jeans, best hiking shoes,
proper flannel, optimum rucksack. It was the 70's.

Did I have these? To splurge we ate at third tier
fast-food joints, our Rambler, a humble brown
to subterfuge rust, best time often spent as a family
was going to the library. My parents were modest,

bordering on pathologically shy. They spoke to each
other in a tongue historically built from sung poetry.
Their American dreams involved praying to all things found
in forests, taking the Tao of suffering and the garden

of never fitting in and building a mysterious melancholy,
sparse beauty found in silence. Where then does capitalism
fit into the life of any child of these people? A junkie
for reverie, sure. An inheritance of paper in all its many forms.

Piles of moldering boxes of music and books left to fend
for themselves amongst basement spiders is their testimony.
If my parents were to share a symbol of a flower
as partners, it would be the waterlily. My father all river,

creek, pond, his name meaning lake, walking hip deep,
boots all mud, focus on beginning, the start of things, the roots.
My mother all upward motion, opening to any damn sun
she could find to speak into the sky, sparks of written word.

Two elements, water to air, their dream.

It is a Flowery Revolution

My mother's garden had a sort of ownership I didn't understand. Mainly because she didn't really share it. Not the planting, the weeding, the feeding or the watering. This was her domain. I was allowed to attend her choices in the nursery. A place of humidity, of humous, imaginable futures. The cloud of scent changed at each turn. Puffs of pollen stuck to your shirt, spilled dirt gunked up your shoes. It was a heady atmosphere that took a gentle hold of the body like a Sloe Gin fizz. Afraid we would miss something important if passing with too much speed, my mother made sure we progressed with all the hurry of the heartbeat of a blue whale. So, we progressed with calculation in mind, checking her internal schematic for what she inked out on her map of hope. I found myself surreptitiously touching all petals, how tender they were, how easy to mush flat. The car would take on the look of an internal parade float. Greenery waved wildly in the warm breeze from open windows. It felt like a holiday. The car often carried silent tongues, some occasional humming, and a boatload of sorrow. I didn't really like my mother's gardens back then. I didn't get it. Other moms had fun, haphazard, running leaps at riots of color; hollyhocks, gladiolas, big maxed-out satisfaction. My mother's garden had a precision of beauty, intricate storytelling, a knowledge about what blends, what harmonizes, what stands alone. Her friend's gardens did their fireworks and smoked out before half the summer was over. My mother's garden was in it for the long haul, laughed right into deep autumn frost. Each spring I head to the garden store acutely aware my mother led me to this, how to cultivate a subtle, verdant depth of field. I also know that back then she was filled to the brim with hot anger- scourge of racism, distant wars killing the children of all her neighbors, women inching toward equal rights and inching back again. And her kneeling in the mud, articulating each wrong into something that started out small, started out green.

To Shine in Answer as My Daughter Goes off to College

I cracked open my motherhood and out flew my daughter
she had wings, a tattoo and was singing *Stoned at the Nail Salon*
Off she went over the pigeons quadrupled up on the freeway lights
to keep warm, those hosts of plague and crispy skin on a skillet

She banked over the single deer self-deposited on the city street
leaping over entire lawns and plastic kid toys
She flew over way too many cornfields, the barometer of America's
love for sweet syrup and Republicans

Slowed her speed over blue highways and pie shops
lazily circled over rivers that once held trout
Hovered over county fairs with carnies that guessed what your kid
after high school, college, military training, band break-ups will do

Past deep forests thick with pine that seem to misdirect,
but really are muses for the natural order of things
She met up with egrets, precise and brilliant,
like if Emily Dickinson could fly

Finally, she entered the time and place of the cicadas
swarms of fat bodies singing their buzzsaws into thick warm air
Telling all about those seventeen years in union with the earth,
waiting, swearing it will be soon, yes it will

Just one more argument with that underground oblivion
before it all split and the hot star poured over every wet wing
And there she landed with her minimalist adult signature
and those piled up years of tender fieldnotes

Common sense words written under
the incandescent lamp of a pandemic
All that to climb out of the complicated casings of childhood
and feel this sun like a thing to eat

a thing to hoard, and enjoy the holy praise
of this newly magnificent din.

Follow the Wild Spill

Her bones remember each hulking woods
as she touches cattail as others touch icons
in an orthodox church, attends cottonwood

release of seed the way some sit
front row at the movies.
What pushed her out of the womb

to meet the natural world in stunned
intoxication once she could pick up rocks?
Let us count back generations to bitchy bogs,

ice blinds, forest spears, naked nests, lonely lichen,
barley flowers, clouds of smelt, milky swans.
Unapologetic, her DNA steers her to mystery snails

in stormy marsh, starburst of mating
dragonflies, dark wisdom in a village of toads.
This is not riddle, but tug and instinct,

raucous and sunstruck, the shimmer and
the hidden, all found in agreeable valleys
up to her neck in the zephyr, the bobolink,

field of cornflowers that take impossible
grieving and convert it into
cold wild song.

Equilibrium

It has been a few years of dodging, hunkering, masking, detaching. Our longitudes lined up in seemingly very wide meridians, lostitudes more like. Daily teachings in the Buddhist concepts of non-grasping, distributed and often not accepted. That sad dance of the non-outreach, the new personal radius spread out like forlorn desert trees, time-out like no one would have ever believed. For some a harsh new chaos theory when trying to pay bills, for others maybe a woolgathering, a discovery of intervals never composed before, a hiatus from the worst kind of work sirocco that flattens all hope, and for some a series of lacunas felt deep in the bones. In my garden, cobwebs pinned to infant birch trees, a bank of wild thyme still hosting bees in a kind of outdoor bar scene, the obscene English cucumbers taunting gravity all along the neighbor's aging fence. We are a country going off like firecrackers and gunshots. A land that is burning, sick and lost in the minimums while those others extract the maximums. In 1852 Thoreau said, "*The ground under the apple tree where we lie, is strewn with small sun-baked apples, but we are not yet reminded of apples.*" In the meantime, we all stumble, everyone trembles. Someday apples will come. But crickets sing, science wants to save our ass, lilies offer sun.

Petrichor smells different on different lands

Remember wet sand, dead bullheads,
Marlboro butts, Coppertone, greasy popcorn,
cherry Chapstick, dried-out honeysuckle, wet

turtles on the beach at sundown. Cool damp
underwear on the line, sun-soaked billowing bras.
Clover rubbed into knees and elbows somersaulting

down the evening hill. The mango, pine, lemon
smoke of weed caught in every seam.
River water skin on skin, lying together naked

in a field of sweet william. Pineapple and rum
of the dark pink crabapple, happy drunk asleep under
blooming lindens. Bright sharp spines of stars

in spruce, boot crunch wintergreen, frost over dream-frog.
Rain on concrete, rain on ponds, rain on any child's hair.
Memory and scent, a catch and release and catch

again. Breathe in, add to the catalog of desire
and fragile detail you carry, a distant whiff of
sometimes a resilient somewhere.

Haikea Longing

Who knows what
the character of any autumn will be?
Sorrow cast in wind and tide of leaf,
weary of the unknown.
Broadcast of goldenrod and aster
and the child that braves thorns,
begs more berries, seed-shot grass
that balance skippers, a back away from
countdown to future equinox as sun dunks
to ebony. The want to remember,
how to step into a summer evening
like it was a great painting, thick-brushed
in green by William Wendt, air pumped
with nicotiana. How this is how it is,
a deep sad need, but not to ruin it,
capture, bottle, place it on a wall.
But let it enter and grow in our bodies
like heartwood.

II

*The waters deep, the waves spread out.
Don't let the dragon get you.*

– Tu Fu

Ice Sings to Itself

> *"American Geophysical Union documents a chaotic low-frequency hum across the Ross Ice Shelf – a platform the size of France that floats off West Antarctica." – Washington Post*

Some say what I emit
is a chaotic rumble
across this shelf, this troubled dune,
warbling for centuries

songs of tonal shifts.
Days and months roll on
between one note,
what's the hurry

in winds that strike my pitch,
notes so low, so slow,
so beyond
the human ear.

But let's remember
who else lives here,
crocodile icefish, sea spiders,
chinstraps, killers, blue-eyed shags,

let's remember
of all that you still do not know
about the sonar of the blue,
about the chilling depths.

I am here, I am not,
carved tunnels of melt
make a crack,
scoring grooves

into a phonograph
Antarctic record, spinning
a cautionary hymn
that turns to flat dial tone

in all the heat.
For these waters
define this tune
on a snow bed dance floor.

Chamber vibrate, channel fluting,
thrum, dirge, drop off.
This is one thin chime
you do not want to hear.

Hesperia Ottoe

The Ottoe Skipper is a critically imperiled and endangered species of butterfly known to have a range from northern Texas to Manitoba.

I feel shy pull
    towards prairie,
        splurge in rye,
at home in bluestem,

though I would burn fast
    like all my cousins
        if set on fire.
Late summer shapes

into profusion,
    then scatter,
        fly-away.
As I wait alone

I ride dried cornhusk
    speed to witchgrass,
        drink blazing star,
bathe in infant gentian.

Thrall under sun,
    subtract in fog,
        hedge the wind,
suckle rain.

I am slow wingbeat,
    slivers left below
        seed-burst
sunflower,

a faint hum
     long after
          song dog
eats big sky.

Baby Rhino
Badlands, South Dakota

Sooner or later the sun
might have found you

where you lay down,
epochs of silts blown away,

wind-devils come to undress
shower of fine particles across

brittle shatters of yourself.
Infant bones undisturbed by nothing

but raptor wing
or stars linked in waves of light.

You passed here with your mother
by cashew and lychee trees,

ferns and bulrushes
along the shallow sea.

To fall,
lost in the circumference

of things to come
by gravity's design,

alongside sea turtles,
buried under ice sheets,

continents birthing mountains,
polar caps, grasslands,

and this sad human
on her hands and knees in clay dust,

your tiny jawbone set into her palm,
splinter of an old wild planet.

Tender message
not yet finished.

Map of Less

Thin thread edge of stream,
    spindles of clay.

Chewed wax of honeycomb,
    weighted sugar in hexagon.

Gray plume of heron,
    wet dagger in cloudburst.

Bulb of thimbleberry,
    juice drop on wasp wing.

Glittering galaxy
    inside fly testicle.

Tiny teeth and inner ear bones,
    snailfish melt-away.

Snowbed willow tree
    tucked into pocket.

Single seafoam shiver,
    one bubble out.

Flowers of watermeal,
    five thousand in a thimble.

Bee Hummingbird egg,
    one coffee bean.

Small god of gnat
    sipping our sorrow.

Tell Me About the Night Flowers

In the gardens of Eudora Welty,
moonflower, gardenia, evening primrose,
tell me how they made their way up in dark,

linked in motions of moon,
petals to shy announcement of scent,
hidden language spoken only to moth.

Tell me about those that ceased from the earth
or to someday turn into metaphor,
cry violet, devil's tongue, false mermaid,
dragon tree, monkey puzzle, holywood.

Tell me how they laced roots in clay,
atomized pollen of golden smoke
stuck to bird belly, to count off
in rain of seeds, promise of serial abundance.

Tell me about it before the clear-cut,
before notion and comfort
hinged hunger to hunger
and trees multiplied secret ecstatic lives.

Tell me about the field
hip deep in sparked beings, monotony
of desire in green wind, tracery shelter
for bone, antenna, whisker, wing.

Tell me how to walk the earth's sunset,
see it fade out, its blended truth
made of many moving parts,
reflection of the injury in forgetting.

Too Warm for the Loon

Winged dart spied
in chunk of liquid sky,
fact and blur.

A haunted song
out of an arsenal
of genius migrations,

spellbound by coy
composition of distance.
Solitary tiny nimbostratus,

slick as a riddle
gothic in its cloak,
arc of language

confessing flight.
Floats in patience, waits
for transit of ice,

the season incognito.
Darkness plus illusion
of every consideration

of the north.
Wandering mirage,
flickering out.

Sea Glossary

To begin with *abyss*
and move to *Aurelia*

        pillow lava, soniferous fish chorus,
        translucent alien jelly falls cascade seafloor

and onto *Bryozoa*,
Cerantium

        crowned branches of lace, beloved of sea spider,
        plant plus animal, red tide water bloom

Dugong,
mermaid, siren

        vulnerable elephant cousin, most needed
        for meat, oil, skin, bones, teeth

Eskimo Curlew,
fat and tender

        shot and dumped two million per year
        in one century. Extinction

Foraminifera,
at death sinks to form beds
of lime to build the Pyramids

        map to locate ancient shorelines,
        track ice ages, find petroleum

Grebe, when startled
will swift dive, not fly

        helldiver, water witch, 400,000
        seabirds a year drowned in gill nets

Hermit Crab,
first advocate of tiny house

        paint your pincer spirit pet, pile them in a pet
        shop tank. Homer Simpson say Hello…Kitty

Icon Seastar,

        cleverly evolved arsenal of hydraulic feet

Juan Fernandez Fur Seal,
>*once four million, great fur coats,*
>*thought extinct, back in delicate balance*

Kittiwake,
>*transatlantic liner gull,*
>*these babies know cliffs*

Longspur,
>*jagged brushstroke in the sky,*
>*all is singing over Arctic water*

Mimic Octopus,
>*dupes predators, queen of impersonation*

Noctiluca,
>*sea sparkles, bioluminescent burglar alarm,*
>*thousands in a single drop of ocean*

Oarweed,
>*devil's apron, sole leather, delicious dashi*

Phalaropes,
>*acre mat of birdwings on the sea,*
>*whale groomers*

Quillfish,
>*sole in species and family, like any writer,*
>*a slender spy*

Radiolaria,
>*Paleozoic exquisite protozoa, star-snowflakes,*
>*secret floaters*

Sea Cucumber,
>*non-sentimental self-preservation, expels innards*
>*to escape enemies, maybe insufferable suitors,*
>*perhaps encroaching fascism*

Turnstone,
>*harlequin stone-flipper, migrant flight wizard*

Unicornfish,
>*scullery maid of coral, mood ring of the waves*

Violet Sea Snail,
>*blind Tiresias, drifts whole life at sea, buoyed on glistening raft of its own bubbles*

Water Boatman,
>*sculling ferryman, sings with its penis*

Xiphosura,
>*horseshoe crab's ten-legged run can't dodge harvesting for fertilizer, biomedical probes*

Yellowlegs,
>*telltale tattler, warns of danger, friend of Aristotle*

Zanizibar Guitarfish,
>*mysterious bluesman of the ocean, rarely caught, life history unknown*

Plentitude times diminishment

>ingenious silver garden

III

We are living in a world of wounds.
– Aldo Leopold

Talking on the Wind Telephone

In a man's backyard in Japan is a telephone booth
Where you can pick up the phone and talk to the dead
To those beloveds who are not here

If I went to this man's phone booth
I would need to bring a tent for all my sorrow
There are many people to call

I would ask my grandmothers
Tell me how you got on that boat and left your homeland
Was doubt a new kind of grief
That sat heavy like a sack of apples at your feet?

I would ask my father to tell me
How it was to be a shy man in a bully land
And how pines are refuge
And fish a coursework on illumination

I would ask my mother
To tell me her dreams
All of them, even the secret ones
That rose up like scent from fiddlehead ferns

I would ask my brother
To tell me the answer to the body breaking down
And how that doesn't stop the birds
From sweeping across the sky

I would ask every singer I have ever loved
How to keep taking deep breaths
Went it hurts, multiply them into stars

I would ask Keats, if he could
Describe trees, the pure breath of sun
Autumn, one more time

I would dial numbers still balanced
On a delicate string of memory
Head down in the act of prayer
And listen

Surviving in a State of Denial

Here is what I do.
Spend days with eggs.
Slip fragile intact blooms
from carton into pot,
let water small tiger purr
to volcanic bubble,
pull off fire,
bathe in ice,
peel insolent shell.

Take good fist
of black dragon oolong,
shallow palm of five spice.
Place in pot of water
immerse eggs into a murk
that clearly has seen corruption
and beauty in all its forms,
boil leaf and set.
Cool with the night.

Next day,
pot back on stove,
boil leaf and set. Cool.
Consider those women poets
who sipped tea alone,
inked chrysanthemums
onto rice paper with
seastar brushes,
waiting.

Third day, three is always good luck,
boil nightmare of black kelp
entwined with aromatic moons,

cool. Remembering:
Darkness within darkness
is the gateway to all understanding.
Slice tea eggs
into lotus flowers,
taste a new dark song –

If one is in exile,
melancholy a river,
take tea and egg
and make a fable.
Feed on
its many echoes.

In the Office of Social Security

There were those glass windows,
openings skulled out for us to speak through,
invitation to get it wrong,
I got it wrong.

The moon would get it wrong,
estimated life expectancy a cyclical calculation,
its chronic disappearance, troubling.
But in this room there was subtraction,

the old man with no legs,
the young man with one arm
and then the woman that entered,
no clothes, no utterance.

When we turned our heads
the policeman covered her
with a raincoat in the vestibule
where she circled slowly on bare feet.

She was kept just outside
the warm government room
filled with people fingering
paper numbers like worry stones.

There is a hard knowledge
in any descent, in the vanishing point
on the cardboard sign of the freeway mendicant,
wedding a blessing of god and hunger

with a magic marker.
We are all lost dogs, riddles, spiders,

all once enchanted children.
Loss is a continuous wheel

that has a difficult spin,
sometimes it cannot stop
once there has been a push off,
a breakaway.

The low roof of the building
was good at stopping rain that day
while we all waited to explain

our willful lack of disappearance,
bowing our heads,
talking through windows.

Olive Trees by Van Gogh

I would take myself
and all those women
visiting their husbands,
sons or daughters in prison,
eating from vending machines,
seated in hard plastic chairs,
children watching cartoons
in the glass room
and put us on a bus.

We would talk of birds,
how long absence sounds
brittle notes, wish phones
spoke more like the sea,
wish voices had
a green taste about them.

We would walk
into the museum
the way clouds
push through sky,
quiet and intent.

We would choose
this idea of wing,
full lush sun,
rescue of leaves
cradling dark fruit,
blue sewn shade.

We would know
how all this works,

the close and the distant,
the heap and faded,
the swoop and the click.

We would feel that paint
press into our own skin,
how it combines, divides.

Who knew that such light
could fit so completely
into the grooves
of all our shadows?

Souvenir
Iceland

It is hard not to take a country
with you when you leave,
mud on treads of shoes,
mineral dust nestled into pores.
It sits in your pockets with sharp rocks
and strange words,
its taste practicing new truths on the tongue,
its rain absorbed where you are thirsty,
the memory of its sun opening you up
like a ripe piece of fruit.

In this country you try to leave something behind.
New grief. You tuck it into your suitcase,
to then try to pack it down with hiking boots
into black lava sand thick as coffee grounds,
toss it out into fields of moss-green boulders
last rolled into place three hundred years before.
Drop it onto hillsides too profuse with wild lupine,
they could surely hold another sad bruise of color.

Release it into the sky with those terns
that circle and dive near your head
as you walk along a shell-crusted path
towards a lighthouse
with the world's smelliest dog
and one lone sheep.

But instead, you and your daughter
place it gently
into the field with the horses
who eat the wildflowers
and the sadness of strangers.

And you sleep the sleep
of a late-setting sun,
a yellow bit of air
you carry in your bones,
a different kind of souvenir.

Walking an Old Dog

There is her gait,
Bone in socket slow,
Joints in solemn protest.

Each step a study of what is still visible,
Each scent an old map,
Each sound distant melody.

Nose lost in soil mound,
A scenery of dreams in leaf pile,
She is your teacher now.

Poet in fur,
Scholar with tail,
Athena with canines.

This is how it is,
The start and stop,
How to perambulate despite loss,

Carve a path in a day that hurts,
Solve the riddle of instinct
To take the leash of another day,

And find that place
Where the dark earth sings
And dig.

Find all that enchants
In the discovered remains
Of one more story.

You know some day this will be you
And you only hope to possess a small part
Of this equanimity

Down under a stand of trees,
The redolent air,
And all those birds.

Ode to Opposite of This

Start with the living,
stand in your own
garden of speculation
where green is alchemy
of hedge and blade.

Kingfisher ready,
skim flint river,
slip inside bulrush, half
hemisphere willow, follow
sun, a heat you had forgotten.

Remember the fluency
of beauty, not just its myth
when it is fugitive.
Pick berries one by one
in a wooded clearing.

Taste their small red hearts,
trick of sugar
inside your body.
Find the balm of denial
in birdsong, wear its pure

motion of dawn.
Take bereavement
with its stealth autumn chill,
tuck it in
with the ditch lilies,

let it lift like spores
into the wind.

IV

I mean those who have trouble fitting in anywhere, those who are on the outside, on the margins.

– Tove Jansson

How to Talk to Introverts

Begin as if it were night
and snow dusts
an overlay of moon
and you don't want to
chase the shadow of a snowshoe hare.

It may appear they are not hearing you,
but they hear more clearly than bats,
better than moths.
They hear wheat grass bending under deer,
the breathing of a shrew.
They are rapt, they are listening.

Sometimes it is better
if there is a tree nearby
or a river with pebbles.
They like presence
of other inventions of the world,
raptures that are not just human.

They are a bit of tumbleweed,
easily pushed by wind,
gather as they go.
When they stop
they have new collections
of loss and dreams.
Sometimes if you ask them
they will tell you about
the drops of dew on the cattail,
the way the orchard grows in silence,
so many apples.

Libraries I Have Known

There was the library with Mrs. Deeble
who knew when a child was in possession
of *The Phantom Tollbooth*,
it was switchback roads of expectations,
brisk verbs embroidering a forest.

There was the one in Italy, atelier
of illuminated words scrimmed in italics,
suspension of disbelief in angel filigree,
dust sat like sacred poems in the corner.

That modern mole hole tucked into the hill,
underground mine of skeptics and tricksters,
graphic novel lounge, cabaret of LP bins
pulsing their own neon.

And the ones that are cloisters for the homeless
sleeping on thin pillows of Popular Mechanics,
sanctuary in the row of lit screens,
heads bent at the precarious altar of Agatha and Sherlock.

And refuge for the immigrant,
children swimming for their new lives in Dr. Seuss,
parents walking alien topography of English dictionaries,
each name on their new card
announcing a deeper citizenship with the word.

There was the one in Helsinki
that closed the doors and locked us in.
That even with the lights turned out
and books absent of a language known to us,
there were still all those volumes attempting
to trim down the barbs of fools
and what better world to be left in and forgotten.

Petites Choses

A button maker
in a small town in England
bakes morsels of clay,
then frees owls and red admirals
onto them from a golden oat brush.

A man in a river town
ties soft hackle flies,
filigree of thread
pushed into slivers of air,
wound into pepper grain knots,
suspicion of bug in tinsel wing.

A family collects
salt grains pushed by tides,
lost waves into flakes.
Gathered and coaxed
into shakers of plentitude,
briny taste of tears.

In an October field of crocus in Iran
women pile open purple
blossoms into buckets,
later to pull each prized filament
as if sewing the air with fine red needles.

Wastepickers accept what is spurned,
sort and bundle the rot and mesh
of our broken
and no longer needed,
intricate coils of copper assemble
before night fall.

We are blind to many things,
ants tucked into winter trees,
hummingbird nests in loops of chain,
pollen moving in sun wind.

Some days we forget
the big loud story
and hunker down,
follow the floating herbs in the soup,
the pointillist way
most of us move through life,
simple dot to simple dot.

 A hand-sewn stitch
crosses all our days,
gathering one small thing
to another.

Girl Monks in Quarantine

Wait as the crocus field
floods hills in purple tide.
It was said if you
ate crocus seeds
on bread, all pain
would disappear.

Our mix of tincture
is found in cloud,
our calligraphy
clicked on screens,
any song born of dawn
chosen by hunger of cat,
heads bowed in entreaty
lost in sudden fog of nap.

But we walk like monks,
our bodies on a wordless
field of green
as branches push bud.

And a new god of sound
in only our foot falls,
scatter of old leaves
repeating the past,

seabird unfurling of curtain,
salutary pot of tea
set upon wooden table,
odes of water
in bucket, in sink, in tub.

Idea of future proofed in
dough puddle, odd prayer
pulled from tired oven.
Mother and daughter,
shy double chorus,
dream, desire, honey, hope.

Cool Cool Water

I found that song
my dad would play
in repetition
on his phonograph

and maybe why
that music unpacked
its bags with him
and took up residence.

He looked into the woods
past his children's eyes
because it was easier
to talk to rain.

Being alone on a river
was another way
he could float above
an absence.

He knew all about barren waste
and how the soul cries out,
he was the shadow
by that big green tree.

I think water
untied his wary tongue,
allowed his failing body
a new map

to that deep channel
of belief and longing,
the liquid prophet
into which he could wade.

Hermit Thrush

Zorzalito Colirrufo
Grive Solitaire

Not lost, not found,
the ground's rough bristle
seals me in
a common precinct.

Tunes thread in patchy light,
rare goods on forest floor.
Try to find the right one
and that is about

how wind fills lungs
and how the belly burns
with the unknown.
I sing to the understory,

to bloodroot and gooseberry,
into dark shadows of trees.
How they sometimes answer,
their branches shedding error

or defeat endured in the day.
Their unburdened shadow
meeting my shadow, maybe
some day meeting yours.

I am Boo Radley

You might say when I lose,
I lose a little bit less of what you lose,
for you say I am not in it full tilt,
my math is not noisy and reckless,
my hungers appear ghostly.
But I do know
shadows are cooling.
They drop their veils
and can unstitch memory
before it is made.
But also, make memory fragrant
and soft as lilacs.
Shadows give space to make a map
in order to navigate what I fear,
what I love that often breaks.
Not that I don't hear every whisper
or know that distance
is another way of being lost.
But being on the outside
has its own power.
There is freedom in a frail world,
you may not see it,
between neither here nor there
this kind of quiet has wings.

V

There is something bigger than fact: the underlying spirit, all it stands for, the mood, the vastness, the wildness.

– Emily Carr

Swim the Compass

Jump out of the canoe,
backstroke that lake,
find that pulse

others carry with them,
those pilgrims of fluent beauty,
that silvery astringent

power scent of youth
that you only feel in water.
Praise the float,

revenge not touching bottom,
all imperfect outsides
now a pale body hum.

This is where you join
your family of swimmers
as if any of your timid ways

mattered any more,
who would know?
All perfect pain kicked off

to drop through layers of waving weeds
past baby bluegills and bounced down
to the mud below to sit with snapping turtles.

To emerge with those
sweet iridescent
satin ribbons of wet,

not yet balanced on land,
but buzzing like a new flower,
facing sun.

The Day Has Wings

In memory of Scott King

You take your shy body
pale voyageur to the knees
through gravity and pull,
surface angel-pinned
all around with dragonflies.

Speech is soft here,
just whir and zip,
humming of all the runes
you have known,
the haibun of turtle,
the canon of cattail,
scripted marsh
chirography.

Here at this floating garden table
you stand and share
the necessity of reflection,
how day builds katydid
and night fades to spore,
how it swirls seed
into this perfect clarity
this small tribe of silver
that lands all around you
like an ancient rain of stars.

Shyland

*The thought of what was here once and is gone forever
will not leave me as long as I live. It is as though
I walk knee deep in its absence. – Wendell Berry*

I

Some say all truths are imperfect,
our landscape docile,
our loss a kind of bluff.
Some say our purpose lies fallow,
it is all too much straw, no silk,
a need and demand for taming,
timid invention too shallow.
There is an elaborate loneliness in bigger roads,
enactments without corona of the whole map,
hungry wounds in mountain spur,
consuming absence of bird song.
Loners of the earth sink themselves
into fog of memory,
but minds and tongues believe in a kind of harvest.
If we name them, the quiet ones,
what kind of spring will follow?
Amnesia has its praises
and a drunken bet pays differently.
If you move in a latitude of victims, whose fault is it?
There is a moon and a kind of drumming,
but which song to sing
to a thin crescent setting?

II

Where are the wild prophets?
Sitting in their canoes, hanging from cliffs,
protesting in Golluk, protecting in Ol Pejeta.
What do we learn from the boneyard,

the darkness down river,
these new locusts sewing blind promises
from deep caves of earth?
Enter the wild horse and course of luna moth,
four deer stopped by the road,
snowy owl, its heart a red jewel beating,
ghost snowprint of rabbit,
their hunger whispering to drifts of stars.
Birds hush to next stunned hush,
now thinning in their wing,
oratory of a different plenitude.

III

Three Kings Kaikomako Tree,
forest of one in the wordless night,
syllables of its cunning green
to share only with ghosts,
solitude in the whine of wind.
The Bristlecone Pine,
Redwood, English Yew,
sunbright wisdom
in their praise of aging.
The Immortal Ones,
Ginkgo, Wollemi Pine, Pando,
labor and psalm of survival beyond
dinosaurs, beyond Black Plague,
rise and fall of empires, Hiroshima.
The odds against the folly,
lies and wishes of us all.

IV

The unclouded wonder, brilliant signal
of a planet spinning in its virtuosity,
a quiet turning in on itself

of all we had, all we need.
Not to toss out the old story,
millennials of branching,
acre upon acre unfolding petals,
promontory of Arctic ice,
rivers of lush transit.
Not to accept that what is left
are curios on dusty shelves,
drawers of lost specimens pinned
with the seductive human desire to count.
Not to dismiss solitary living
in all its many shy forms,
pocket mouse in sage scrub,
emerald dragonfly by
one white fawnlily.

V

Not to overlook
if any of them will stay
or where any of them will go.
Not to forget the great arc
of all the living,
the heartbreaking,
rapt bloom
of it all.

Koivu

but then I will no longer be me,
but the forest. - Eeva-Liisa Manner

It wasn't a music room,
but it had that same unscrolling of subtle notes
that hang in the air, that change your breathing.

It wasn't a church,
but there was a query of spirit
in the way of prayers waving.

It wasn't a boat house,
yet water was clearly part of its desire,
a deep secretive thirst lifted through the bones.

It wasn't a season,
but it did invite green singing of birds,
seemed to intend that yellow be the color
we slip over any new sorrow.

It wasn't immortal,
but being there beside it made you feel
like a certain kind of labor took place
you will never come to understand,
an unequivocal wisdom, a language unknown.

It wasn't a bridge,
yet any child knew an invitation was being offered,
connecting one world to another.

It was a birch tree,
planted by a forty-five-year-old man
on a slight hill in his suburban front yard,

answering the call of his ancestors
four thousand miles away

who were known to take the bark
to soften into the shape of shoes,
bundle tiny spring leaves to set over hot rocks,
drink the sap in a healing tea.

My father dug a birch tree hole,
his body remembering
something long lost
as he knelt there in the dirt.

And he filled it
with expectation of something bigger,
something fluent,
a bit of myth to pass by each day
on his way to work.
Something pure,
something gone wild.

Baptism River

As if it knows the sun
is a thing that points out

complacency,
cold lips of water

roll over floating marigolds
a supple telling of how

the wet world opens
and closes.

Silver rapids beat
half rhymes

into stone
with new strung verbs,

slippery litanies
in how it frills out matter,

refashions hunger,
hands back moonlight.

Particles, atoms and elements
stirred inside its fluid tongue,

to pour it all over ice,
dump it like the magnanimous

instrument of jamboree it is,
droplet and surge, sober and wild.

How it keeps telling us
to get over it already,

more pain and stories
and dreams to come,

how past swirls and collects
how future spills on.

Acknowledgements

This book began as a conversation. For three months in 2020, I read each day from *The Journal of Henry David Thoreau* Volumes I-XIV published by Dover Press. I took a daily walk and wrote a response. The poems in the first and last section of this book are from those responses. The other poems are also conversations -with my family, my heritage, with the natural world and its *panorama of endless change* as Rachel Carson called it. And also, poems about loss, subtraction, and introversion. Shy has always been a kind of minus in this culture, a choice to be less, a diagnosis. In rejecting the shy in human and land, there is only more loss. A part of being human as Ursula Le Guin said, *involves acceptance of impermanence and imperfection… a friendship with water, darkness, and the earth.* Looking for that patience as we all stumble and discover.

These poems were previously published, some in earlier forms.

"Ode to the Opposite of This"
Kippis, Nordic Journal

"The Day Has Wings"
I'll Try to Save This Place, supersessionspress

"Girl Monks in Quarantine"
Artistic Antidote to COVID-19- University of Minnesota, Academic Clinical Affairs

"Down to Earth", "Again the Doves in the Time of the Pandemic", "Hermit Thrush", "Too Warm for the Loon"
Little by Little, The Bird Build's His Nest: A Poetry Anthology – Paris Morning Publications

Thank you to all who have been instrumental in helping a shy poet work on this group of poems that evolved into *Shy Lands*. A special thank you to Pat Barone and Kate Dayton who have been unfailing supporters of all my work over the years and helped make sure these poems became a book. To John Reinhard and all the poets in his cross-country poetry newsletter, witness to all these poems in their embryonic form. To Scott King who gave me those two Dover journals of Thoreau and guided me to all the many environmental shy lands of his studies. We miss you and you guide us still. To Diane Raptosh who urged me to keep going when I wasn't sure this was any kind of book. To the ESAC Poets who always inspire me. To the poets in memory care, adult day and assisted living, who show me the luminous in any part of a day. And to my daughter LiLi, my wise walking companion through life and explorer of all the beauties that still thrive on this planet.

About the Author

Diane Jarvenpa is the author of *The Way She Told her Story*, *The Tender Wild Things* and *Divining the Landscape* -New Rivers Press and *swift, bright, drift* and *Ancient Wonders, The Modern World*- Red Dragonfly Press. She has received The Midwest Independent Publishers Association Award and an Artist Initiative grant from the Minnesota State Arts Board. She is a teaching artist with the Alzheimer's Poetry Project MN and St Paul's East Side Arts Council. She was awarded a grant to produce a film using poems from her book *The Way She Told Her Story* together with songs from her CD *Bittersweet*. As a singer-songwriter performing under the name Diane Jarvi, she has seven recordings and was awarded a Minnesota Arts and Cultural Fund grant and received a McKnight MacPhail performing fellowship.

www.dianejarvi.com

About the Author

Diane Jarvenpa is the author of *The Way She Told her Story*, *The Tender Wild Things* and *Divining the Landscape* -New Rivers Press and *swift, bright, drift* and *Ancient Wonders, The Modern World*- Red Dragonfly Press. She has received The Midwest Independent Publishers Association Award and an Artist Initiative grant from the Minnesota State Arts Board. She is a teaching artist with the Alzheimer's Poetry Project MN and St Paul's East Side Arts Council. She was awarded a grant to produce a film using poems from her book *The Way She Told Her Story* together with songs from her CD *Bittersweet*. As a singer-songwriter performing under the name Diane Jarvi, she has seven recordings and was awarded a Minnesota Arts and Cultural Fund grant and received a McKnight MacPhail performing fellowship.

www.dianejarvi.com

www.ingramcontent.com/pod-product-compliance
Lightning Source LLC
Chambersburg PA
CBHW031203160426
43193CB00008B/485